CW01659270

Faith

Margaret Silf

DARTON·LONGMAN+TODD

First published in 2011 by
Darton, Longman and Todd Ltd
1 Spencer Court
140 – 142 Wandsworth High Street
London SW18 4JJ

ISBN: 978-0-232-52794-0

A catalogue record for this book is available from the British Library.

Phototypeset by Judy Linard
Printed and bound in Great Britain by Thomson Litho, East Kilbride, Scotland

Contents

	Introduction	5
1	*Who is God for me?*	7
2	*Relating to God*	11
3	*'God is love' – could this be true?*	15
4	*Certainty or Mystery?*	19
5	*Does life have any meaning?*	23
6	*Where is my life centred?*	27
7	*Who is Jesus?*	31
8	*Following Jesus*	35
9	*Entering the Gospels in prayer*	39
10	*Can my life make any difference?*	43
11	*Faith is as faith does*	47
12	*Journeying alone, journeying together*	51
13	*I want to ask God …*	55
14	*I need to ask myself …*	59
15	*I believe …*	63

Introduction

My baby granddaughter has more faith than I do.

She believes that when I am holding her I won't drop her.

She believes that when she is hungry someone will feed her.

She believes that life and the world mean well with her.

She believes – indeed I hope she knows – that we love her.

She doesn't think about 'faith'. She just lives it.

As she grows older her faith will get more complicated.

She will learn that sometimes life will let her down and she will get hurt.

She will discover that not every need is going to be met, just because she shouts loudly enough.

She will learn to distinguish between those things in life – like kindness, compassion, justice and truth – that are making her, and all of us, more fully alive, and those things – like war and greed and selfishness – that are working against that fullness of life.

She will come to understand that faith is a cooperative venture, and that her own actions and choices will have reactions and results.

She will try to work things out, try to pin things down and get a grasp on her life's meaning.

She will hear many conflicting voices and may come to think that 'faith' is hard work, an intellectual marathon, a puzzle to be gnawed at until a solution emerges.

Then one day, please God, she will become older and wiser. By then she will have learned that the hurts along the way will have made her stronger, clarified her inner truth, revealed her own limitations.

She will concede that sometimes, after all, God knew best, and that good things grow from seeds that have been broken open by the weather and lain hidden in the dark earth. She will look back over the kaleidoscope of her life and notice how the fragments of experience that made no sense at the time are shaping a rather beautiful pattern.

What faith she has then will be simple again. But it will have the simplicity born of experience and reflection – a simplicity that looks back with gratitude on all she has seen and done and lived, and is confident in trusting God for all that remains unseen, undone, unlived. It will be the kind of faith that knows that God is more likely to ask her, at the end of her journey, 'How well did you love?' than 'How much did you understand?' And her answer might be:

Someone trusted me and I didn't let them down.

Someone was hungry and I fed them.

Someone was hopeless and I gave them a reason to trust that at least one person meant well with them.

Someone had no one, and I loved them.

It sounds simple.

But it takes a lifetime to reach that simplicity, and to come full circle, from infant faith to mature faith, from the source of our being to its destiny.

Simple faith is simply to journey in trust, like a baby, but with the wounds and scars of an adult, like a man who died on a cross, and invites us to 'become like little children', and when we follow him we discover that his footsteps lead right back, full circle, to a whole new beginning.

1

Who is God for me?

A LITTLE GIRL IN kindergarten was painting a picture. Her teacher asked her: 'What are you painting?' The child replied: 'It's a picture of God.' Very interested to see what the result would be, the teacher commented: 'But nobody knows what God looks like.' 'They will when I have finished my picture,' replied the child confidently.

We all have our 'pictures of God', and most of them started to form in early childhood. Of course no one has seen God. So it follows that any picture, or image, of God that we may form is going to be completely inadequate, and may even be seriously harmful.

Some of the unhelpful images we commonly have of God include:

- God the strict parent or school teacher, waiting to catch us out in wrongdoing and punish us;
- God the fireman, who comes to the rescue when we are in trouble;
- God the Santa Claus who delivers the items on our wish list;
- God who fights on our side in every battle and vanquishes our enemies;

- God the demanding employer who expects us to work all hours and rarely gives us a bonus.

All these have one thing in common: they image God as a person, like us, only bigger and more powerful. Because we are human, it's inevitable that, like the little girl, we will make pictures of God that look like ourselves, since this is all we know. But could we do better than this? Can our image of God grow up a bit, now we are grown up ourselves?

Some alternative images ...

Mystics through the ages have struggled to express their sense of God in more abstract ways, for example:

- The word who calls creation into being;
- The energy of all life;
- The deep wisdom underlying all that exists;
- The spirit that holds us in being and guides us;
- The light in which all is known and understood and which outshines all our shadows.

Quakers speak of 'that which is of God within all beings'.

Anthony de Mello tells the story of the fish that was searching for the mystery he called 'Ocean'. 'Where is Ocean?' he asked every other fish he met. Nobody could tell him. 'What does Ocean look like?' Nobody could say; nobody had ever seen it.

Perhaps the fish went on his way, dismissing the idea of 'Ocean' as a figment of the collective imagination.

Or perhaps he realised that 'Ocean' was the fullness of the mystery in which he and all the creatures of the deep live and move and have their being.

Many people would dismiss the idea of 'God' as a fiction.

Others intuit that God is the mystery in which we all live and move and have our being.

Do I believe ...?

To be a person of faith is to believe that there is a power greater than ourselves, an all-powerful mystery in whom we live and move and have our being.

For the fish, the ocean is the medium that holds it afloat, that nourishes it and, by means of subtle movements and currents, guides its path. If the fish could leap out of the ocean it would die. It isn't actually possible to leap out of the medium in which we have our being.

Nor is it possible to reject the reality of the mystery we call 'God'. But it is possible, and sometimes necessary, to reject our own flawed and damaging images of God.

Try taking stock of some of your own images of God.

Are there any you feel you need to let go of?

Is there any image that really works for you?

Images can be helpful, but they are only images, only a human attempt to describe what cannot be described. Let them help you in your faith journey, but don't let them imprison you.

A person of faith is someone who knows that he or she is not the centre of the universe, but acknowledges that this centre of gravity lies in a mystery much deeper than human hearts can fathom – a mystery we call 'God'.

What do you think?

When you say: 'I believe in God', what do you mean?

> God said to Moses, 'I AM WHO I AM'
>
> EXODUS 3:13

2

Relating to God

HUMAN BEINGS, LIKE all mammals, are conceived, born and live their lives in relationship. We are each a part of a vast and inter-dependent web of life, in which every individual finds his or her meaning in the context of the whole.

We all know how challenging it can be to live in healthy and loving relationships with each other. Relating to each other is the most demanding aspect of what it means to be human, but it is at the very heart of what makes us human.

If God is the mystery in whom this web of life has its being, then God is surely also longing to be in relationship with each of us, and with all of us. How might this work?

Relationship is a two-way street.

God wants to reveal Godself to us.

We want to find a meaningful relationship with God.

Such a two-way relationship, like any human relationship, will involve some self-disclosure.

God will reveal something of God's nature to us.

We are invited to share ourselves and our concerns with God.

A person of faith is one who tries to read the meanings of God in our world, and desires to respond to these meanings in a way that best expresses his or her own personality.

How could this work?

For as long as human beings have been around on this planet, they have tried to find ways of being in relationship with God. They have discovered, for example, that something of the nature of God is revealed through:

- The created world
- Sacred scripture
- The story of the universe
- The lives of people who have lived close to the heart of God
- The events of our everyday lives
- Our human relationships.

Creation itself is covered with the footprints of the creator.

It shows us the delicate dance between light and darkness, action and rest, life and death. It tells us the story of how our universe began and how it is sustained in being, in spite of our own thoughtless lifestyles.

Sacred scripture tells another story – of how we have tried to listen to God's voice through our human history. It invites us to hear God's meanings through historical accounts, through parable, through story and in words of wisdom.

Other people show us how they have learned to relate to God and follow where God leads, and their stories invite us to learn from them and follow the ways of truth and love along with them.

And God is right there in our ordinary days and weeks, our conversations and interactions, our sorrows and our joys, waiting to be recognised.

And our response?

We can begin to cultivate a relationship with God in much the same way we would with another human being.

We can share our thoughts, our fears, our joys and our sorrows, our hopes and our dreams, in the dialogue we call 'prayer'.

It isn't so hard.

When we express the things we feel most deeply, in the quiet of prayer, we are not really 'telling God' our concerns, but bringing them to mind ourselves, in the conscious presence of God.

You could say that we are bringing them into a sharper focus, in the light of God's love, exposing them to the beam of that love, whether we are praying for ourselves or for someone else.

We can develop this relationship by living in daily awareness of what is actually going on in our lives, and learning to notice those moments when we feel God is close, perhaps suggesting new directions or calming long-standing fears, or opening our hearts to moments of joy in the presence of great beauty or incidents that move us deeply.

Every movement in our hearts is an invitation to respond to God's action in our lives. Every day we live has the potential to take us a little bit further in our desire to relate to the mystery of God.

What do you *think?*

Genuine relationship, whether with each other or with God, depends on whether we want to be in relationship.

If the desire is there, the rest will follow.

What is your desire?

In what special ways do you feel God expresses Godself to you?

How do you respond?

> 'Every happening, great and small, is a parable whereby God speaks to us, and the art of life is to get the message.'
>
> MALCOLM MUGGERIDGE

3

'God is love' – could this be true?

ALBERT EINSTEIN ONCE said that the most important question we could ever ask is: 'Does the universe mean well with us'?

The question may surprise, and even shock some Christians.

Or perhaps it is another way of asking, can we really believe that 'God is Love'?

If you were to ask a random sample of people in the street whether they think the universe is ultimately benevolent, neutral or hostile towards us, you would probably find that the majority would think the universe is neutral – that it doesn't 'care' what becomes of us.

Perhaps you feel like that yourself, especially when you think of all the problems that life poses.

And yet people of faith have consistently claimed that 'God is love'. Is it just a cliché? Or could it possibly be true?

When we tell our children 'God loves you', do we believe it ourselves?

It's often hard to think of ourselves as being 'lovable' at all. Maybe we haven't experienced much love in our younger lives. Maybe we have been subjected to a lot of destructive criticism. Maybe we have begun to think that we are not worth much, and why would anyone, let alone God, love us?

Maybe, if we are really honest we are not totally convinced ourselves. God may be a God of love in theory, but could God possibly love me?

Two witnesses for the defence

God doesn't need defending, of course, any more than the ocean needs to justify itself to the fish.

But sometimes we need convincing.

What convinces me that God is love?

My first witness is my own memory bank.

There have been times in the past – maybe only a very few times, and very rare moments, but no less real and vivid for all that – when I felt, with absolute clarity, the sense of God touching my life in some way.

Perhaps moments when I felt deeply at one with the created world or with another human being.

Or moments when I felt powerfully guided in some way.

Or profoundly comforted in some distress...

When I recall such moments, do I feel that God's touch upon my life was a loving touch?

The answer, for me, is a resounding: Yes! It was always a loving touch, though frequently also a very challenging touch.

My second witness is Jesus of Nazareth, whom Christians believe to be a unique manifestation of God in human form.

How did Jesus touch the lives of those around him?

Was it with love, or was it neutral, or even hostile?

I don't think even the fiercest detractors of Christianity would suggest that Jesus' actions were ever 'neutral'!

No! Jesus went about his world touching people with healing, with life, with new hope and with compassion, though that touch too was often very challenging.

Love ... from Day One?

Scientists tell us that at the very beginning of our universe, there was a slight imbalance between 'particles' and 'anti-particles'. We don't need to know what particles and anti-particles are to understand that this tiny imbalance was what led to the possibility of life. The fact is that when a particle meets an anti-particle they mutually destroy each other. Had there been no imbalance, there would have been no universe, no earth, no you or me. The imbalance was minute, but it was in favour of the particles. Those particles that survived eventually became the primeval components of life.

I would call that a universe that actively desires life.

I would call that a God who is striving, constantly, even from Day One, to bring forth life-in-all-its-fullness.

And there are a host of other examples in science, where a tiny imbalance in favour of what leads to life made all the difference.

So, I believe ...

That at the heart of all that is, is a mystery I call God.

And that this mystery is intentional.

Its intention is always to bring forth the more life-giving outcome, in the story of creation just as in the story of each one of us.

It is a loving intention, and a personal intention.

And therefore, though God is clearly not a person like us, just bigger and better, God is a personal power, with an overwhelmingly loving intention towards all creation and to each creature, including, even, me.

What do you *think?*

What evidence do you find in your own life that God's touch is a touch of love?

When you say 'God is love', can you believe it?

> 'I am a little pencil in the hand of a writing God who is sending a love letter to the world.'
>
> MOTHER TERESA OF CALCUTTA

4

Certainty or Mystery?

ALICE IN Alice in Wonderland complains about the demand on her to 'believe six impossible things before breakfast'. For many people the process of initiation into a religious tradition might feel rather like this. Candidates for baptism or confirmation, for example, might be required to undergo some significant period of tuition about the doctrinal propositions to which they will be required to assent.

In some cultures this tuition begins with the very young and takes the form of a 'catechism' of the tenets of the faith, which they will learn by heart, not always with any degree of real understanding. Latterly, however, this process has often been superseded by a more enlightened guided journey of discovery into what the life of faith, within a particular tradition, might mean.

This change in itself highlights the challenging question: 'Am I yearning for certainty, or am I open to the risk of mystery? Do I see faith as a set of absolute beliefs with which I can agree, or is faith for me more like a journey of discovery, drawing me constantly beyond all my limited 'certainties' towards a mystery that will always lie beyond my understanding?

A related question might also be: If I align myself to

a faith community, am I joining a members-only organisation, or do I see myself rather as part of an adventure that welcomes every searching heart?

Some thoughts to ponder …

We often hear that religion causes much of the world's conflicts.

If this is so, why might it be?

You may have heard about the three people who all claimed to have seen God. They began to argue about how God looked and what God was wearing – especially, they argued about the colour of God's hat. One swore that it was a red hat. The other had seen a yellow hat. The third was totally convinced that God's hat was blue. What none of them realised was that God's hat was a rainbow hat, with a different colour shining out from every angle.

If they had been able to sit more lightly to their imagined certainties, they might have avoided conflict, and in fact come to learn a lot from each other, which would have enriched them all.

Of course, the colour of God's hat is a trivial fiction.

Our certainties become much more damaging when we convince ourselves that certain tenets about faith are absolute, and then try to impose them on others, who will have a different set of 'certainties.' It isn't hard to see where this kind of fundamentalism is leading us.

Certainty divides us.

Mystery unites us.

Bubbles and basilicas

I was once sitting in a little park in the small town of Loyola in Spain. Behind me was the imposing basilica of St Ignatius, who was born there, an edifice that at that time was covered in scaffolding and under renovation. In front of me was a small kiosk selling newspapers, chocolate and other small items.

A man came along, with his small daughter and their dog. The man bought a newspaper for himself and a little container of soap bubbles for his small daughter to play with. They sat down beside me. The man was engrossed in his newspaper. The little girl was delightedly blowing soap bubbles, clearly entranced by the magical coloured globe that each bubble formed as it caught the sunlight. The dog jumped up after every bubble and tried to catch it but as soon as he seized the bubble with his snout, the bubble burst.

I asked myself, which is teaching me more about the kingdom of God – the mighty basilica with all its scaffolding, or this little girl's joy at the beauty of the world reflected in her bubbles. And the little dog taught me that as soon as we try to take hold of the mystery, and pin it down into our own categories, words and meanings, we destroy it.

If we think we have 'got' it, we will lose it.

If we think we have 'arrived', we have gone down a cul-de-sac.

What do you *think?*

The idea of 'God' is a concept that will always lie beyond the grasp of limited, time-bound human minds. God will always be a mystery. If the reality we call God were not a mystery it would not be God.

How do you feel about living, and growing within this mystery that will defy all your attempts to fit it into human categories?

> 'True faith is a leap away from fossilised beliefs into the mystery of the Unknown God ...'
>
> KIERKEGAARD

5

Does life have any meaning?

THERE IS A big divide between people who regard life as a random event in a random universe, with no inherent meaning, and those who believe that their life's journey, and the journey of all humanity, has real meaning and purpose.

Perhaps there is no answer.

But to be a person of faith is to come down on the side of meaning.

And our deep desire to discover meaning in life might in itself be a sign that there is meaning to be discovered.

Most religions are attempts to formulate the meaning of life in terms of a particular understanding of God. But do those formulations really satisfy our heart's searching? To be truly convinced that life has meaning and purpose, perhaps we need to search our own experience first, because any sense of purpose will be personal, before it becomes universal.

In today's world it is easy to despair of any progress in our human journey. The news headlines emphasise the opposite kind of movement – a regression, rather than a progression, and the return of chaos rather than a growth towards a higher and more compassionate order.

So which is right: the voice of despair or the voice of hope? Resignation to the apparent disintegration of society, or the desire to turn things in a different direction?

So what is *it all about?*

A friend sent me a joke card with the caption: 'What if the hokey cokey really is what it's all about?'

Fair question. But the same friend who sent the card spends her own life, unstintingly, in caring for young children. Her life has meaning. More than the hokey cokey, I would suggest.

So what could the purpose of our existence really be? Everyone would have a different answer, and certainly no-one would have the definitive answer.

But our desires give us some clues.

At the turn of the millennium, global television followed the dawn of the new era through all the world's time zones, and everywhere the hopes and dreams that were expressed were the same: for peace. Not just the absence of conflict, but the deep wholeness of things expressed in the Hebrew word 'shalom'.

Could this be an indication of life's meaning?

To become, individually and collectively, the best that we can be?

To build a society where everyone can live in freedom and in peace?

To evolve over time into the higher levels of

consciousness where compassion would prevail over egotism, and co-operation over competition?

In short, the kind of world for which Jesus himself lived, and died?

What is my role in the journey?

A traveller once went into a little shop. The shop-keeper asked him: 'What would you like? We have everything here that you could desire.' The traveller's reply came promptly:

> I would like a world where all can live in peace; where everyone has enough to eat and every child can go to school. I want a world where everyone looks out for their neighbour and cares for others as much as for their own kith and kin.

At this point the shopkeeper interrupted: 'Sorry sir. I forgot to mention: we don't sell the fruits here; we only sell the seeds.'

If we believe that life has meaning and purpose, we can make our dreams a reality. We can, and must, become the change we want to see.

It won't happen on its own. It won't grow unless we plant the seeds.

So our role is very clear.

Each of us, we believe as people of faith, carries a

seed of God's Kingdom – something that only we can plant and nurture, each of us uniquely.

The challenge is to recognise the particular way in which we can personally help to nudge the human family a little bit closer to God's dream for 'shalom'.

If we believe that we are part of a journey that has meaning and purpose, how are we going to make that journey a reality?

What do you *think?*

Is there a reason why you are here?

What kind of special seed can your life sow into the field of human growth?

How are you going to nourish it?

'Tell me, what is it you plan to do with your one wild and precious life?'

MARY OLIVER

'Let us endeavour so to live that when we come to die even the undertaker will be sorry.'

MARK TWAIN

6

Where is my life centred?

ONLY A FEW hundred years ago most people were completely convinced that planet Earth was the centre of the entire universe. And since they also thought human beings were the pinnacle and ultimate purpose of creation on Earth, then it followed that humankind was at the centre of the universe, and therefore free to exploit creation as we wished.

Now, with the benefit of all our technology and our increasing understanding of the origins of our universe, we flinch at such arrogance. And yet we tend to live our daily lives as though nothing has changed – as though human needs always take precedence over the needs of our planet, and as though our personal desires or those of our family or our tribe go ahead of the needs of the rest of creation.

The result of everyone thinking and acting as though creation revolves around themselves is obvious: rivalry, mutual distrust, conflict and war – the very opposite of the deep human longing for 'shalom'. The 'centre of gravity' lies in ourselves and our egos, and everything else has to come into orbit around that ego-centre.

The truth is, of course, that the centre of gravity of creation lies much deeper than in any individual need or requirement. The universe revolves around the balance of life itself. For this balance to be maintained, every living thing has to live in harmony with that reality, or else be in perpetual conflict. It isn't hard to see which option the human race has tended to choose so far.

A different way ...?

But there is another way. In fact the people we most revere in the human story are usually those who have chosen to walk to the beat of a different drum, challenging us to find other, less ego-centric ways of relating to God and to each other.

We rate altruism high on the scale of human values, and we deplore selfishness. This way of seeing things finds expression in the spiritual precept, found in different forms of words in most religious traditions, that we often call the Golden Rule:

> 'Love your neighbour as you love yourself. Behave towards others in the way you would wish them to behave towards you.'

We sense intuitively, and we try to teach our children, that we should put the greater good before our own personal benefit, but the ego fights back – hard! We can find ourselves swimming against the currents of a 'me-first' society and the attitudes of our contemporary culture. We also find it surprisingly hard to 'love ourselves', as the Golden Rule calls us to do.

To be a person of faith is to make a choice to centre one's life around the deeper centre of gravity we call God, and the greater good of all creation, rather than primarily around one's own personal gain and benefit. It is to act with loving-kindness, to ourselves and to each other.

How can we do this in practice?

It sounds easy and obvious, but in practice it is very difficult to maintain this deeper focus.

One problem we have in turning the ideal into the real is that we try to leap across the miles instead of navigating the inches. We are not asked to save the world or redeem the universe, but only to take each next step with regard for this deeper centre of gravity that holds us in balance with the Golden Rule.

A very helpful and practical way to do this is by using this kind of reflective prayer (often called the Review prayer, or the Examen)...

Take a short time, about 10 to 15 minutes, ideally each day, just to play back to yourself what has actually happened during the day, how you felt about it and how you reacted. Ask yourself: 'What happened today to make me feel more alive, more truly myself, more grounded in the centre of my being?' 'What happened today for which I want to say 'Thank you'?' 'Did I do or say anything today for which I feel regret?'

Notice very specially any memories that surface that cause a strong reaction in you – perhaps joy or gratitude, or anger, regret or some kind of inner disturbance. These 'hot spots' are indicators that these parts of your day's experience are important, and have something to show you about the deepest movements of your heart.

What do you think?

You have probably made a deep and lifelong commitment to try to live from your own deepest centre in God, when you committed yourself to a life of faith. However, there will be moments every day when you will temporarily turn away from this deep commitment, in pursuance of your own more ego-centred interests.

Try using the Review prayer to check out those turnings and re-turnings, and notice their root causes in your own lived experience.

Make a note of any parts of that experience where you feel you tend to follow the ego, and any parts that tend to be more deeply grounded in your true centre, where God is indwelling.

> 'Everyone must decide whether to walk in the light of creative altruism or in the darkness of destructive selfishness.'
>
> MARTIN LUTHER KING

7

Who is Jesus?

TWO THOUSAND YEARS ago, in a remote village in the Middle East, a child was born who was destined to turn the world around.

Plenty of people have tried to define who he was, and the nature of his personhood. There is no shortage of doctrines surrounding the question of who we think he was, and is.

Faith tells me that this man is the person I need to follow; the person who for me reveals everything that humanity is called to become – everything that God is dreaming we can become. He shows us what our humanity can look like when it is fully evolved. He also shows us the cost of following the path that leads us to this fulfilment of who we are.

Faith tells me this.

Simple faith tells me that if I truly want to follow him, I don't need to get tangled up in all the (sometimes conflicting) theories and doctrines about him.

All kinds of different people were attracted to Jesus' teaching when he lived on earth. Many were simple, illiterate peasants, who apparently had no problem in understanding and responding to him. Others were highly educated people. Some were models of good behaviour, exemplary in their religious practice. Others were a mess, and knew it. It clearly didn't require a doctorate in theology to follow this man. In fact too much head learning, and certainly too much 'righteousness', appear to have been more of a hindrance than a help along the way.

So what can we say about him?

We know some basic facts about Jesus from independent historical accounts from the time of his earthly lifetime. That he lived in Israel and was executed for alleged sedition are historical facts beyond reasonable dispute.

But Christians believe a lot more about him than these bare facts.

We believe that he shows us, in a unique way, what the fullness of God's love is like when it takes human form.

We believe that he incarnates that 'word' that underpins all creation, and that 'light' that reveals not only the divine glory but the depth of our shadows as well.

We believe that he shows us not only the goal of our human journey, but also the cost of its fulfilment.

We believe that he shows us through his teachings and his life what it means to live by a completely different set of values from those that normally prevail in our present societies and personal lives.

We believe that when he died, his essential spirit was released in a way that liberated the pure energy of God in what we call the Holy Spirit, and that this energy empowers us to follow Jesus in our own living. Because of this, we believe that Jesus has truly transcended what our human understanding sees as 'death'.

The heart of the matter

It's very hard to know for sure exactly what Jesus said and did during his life on earth. But we do have four accounts of his life, death and resurrection in the four Gospels that were selected to be included in our New Testament scriptures.

At the very heart of these accounts is the astonishing challenge of what we call The Beatitudes. These blessings of Jesus to his followers turn all our expectations on their heads. They tell us, in different ways, that it is those who appear to have nothing, those in grief, those in poverty, those who are maligned and persecuted, the meek and the gentle, who are closest to the real core of what it means to be truly human. Only when we have nothing left to lose can we discover the core of who we really are. Only when we allow God to upturn our self-focused values will we see where our true destiny is leading us.

Such teaching might well fill us with fear. How can we possibly live like that? Jesus' answer is clear, and frequently repeated:

'Don't be afraid!'

He doesn't just say it, or preach it or teach it.

He lives it, by living totally true to God's dream, regardless of the cost.

He dies it, freely allowing the powers of darkness to destroy him.

And then he transcends it, releasing the power of his whole being to flow through all those who follow after him.

Who is Jesus for you?

Jesus once asked his friends the question:

'Who do you say that I am?'

If he were to ask you this question, how would you respond?

> 'Jesus is God spelling Himself out in language that man can understand.'
>
> S. D. GORDON
>
> 'He changed sunset into sunrise.'
>
> CLEMENT OF ALEXANDRIA

8

Following Jesus?

The Invitation

Again and again in the Gospels, Jesus issues the invitation to 'Follow me'. He doesn't say 'Worship me'. He doesn't say 'Go to church'. He says: 'Follow me', 'Trust me' and, over and over, 'Don't be afraid.'

When he is asked, by John's disciples (John 1: 39), 'Where do you live? What are you about? What makes you tick?' He doesn't give an answer, but an invitation: 'Come and see.' He invites us to make a journey of discovery – discovering who we are and who we can become, who our 'neighbour' is, who Jesus is, and who God is for us.

To follow Jesus is to hear and respond to this invitation, to follow, to come and see for ourselves who he is for us and what his presence in our hearts is asking of us in our world today.

Sometimes that 'follow me' is a daunting challenge. For example, he also invites people to leave behind what they have been doing so far, or at least the ways they have been doing it, to let go of their old securities, even their old way of life, and to set out on a road that has no signposts, but only a travelling-companion who is waiting to accompany and guide us step by step.

Because it is so challenging and frightening, Jesus urges his companions, time and time again, not to be afraid. Fear is our worst enemy when it comes to responding to this invitation to become 'people of the Way'. Jesus takes the fear head-on, and leads us beyond it, if we really dare to follow.

The Way

So, what is this 'way' we are invited to walk?

It is the Way of Love. Jesus tells us not only to 'love our neighbour', but also to 'love our enemies', and, maybe hardest of all, 'to love ourselves'. How do we generate this 'love' when we maybe don't feel loving at all? I find the words of M. Scott Peck very helpful here. He reminds us that 'Love is not an emotion. Love is a decision.' So what Jesus is asking of us is not to feel loving to everyone we meet, but freely to choose to do the most loving, the most life-giving thing in every situation. This puts a rather different slant on it. The impossible becomes a little bit more possible. We can't control how we feel, but we can choose how we act and what we say in every situation. We can choose our attitude towards the people we meet. We can choose generosity over spitefulness, an encouraging word over a sarcastic remark.

It is the Way of Truth. Jesus asks us, in every situation to act and speak in a way that rings true at the core of our being – to do the right thing, not in hope of any reward, or from fear of any punishment, but simply because it is the right thing, the more loving thing to do, in that situation. He doesn't just ask this of us, he shows us in every action and choice of his own life, what it looks like to live completely true to the core of our being where God is indwelling. He calls us to 'do as I do', and take into ourselves the values and attitudes that his own life reveals, seeking to make them our own.

It is the Way of Life. If we dare to walk it, we will discover that it leads to 'life in all its fullness.' It invites us to become human beings fully alive.

The Cost

When you really live true to the very best in yourself, perhaps by speaking out against injustice or stating your truth in a hostile situation, you will provoke a reaction. Even a small remark that challenges unacceptable behaviour can bring down a very violent response.

Jesus is the one who lives completely true to the Father's dream for humanity. He shines like a light in the darkness. But that light provokes the darkness and the darkness rises up to swallow and apparently destroy him. He is executed because he is a constant 'threat to national security' and also a thorn in the flesh of the religious authorities. He warns his followers that they too will be 'crucified' in some form if they live true to his teachings. If you have ever spoken out about some issue in your own situations, including religious issues, you will have experienced something of what it means to 'take up your cross and follow me.'

Jesus knows very well what the consequences will be for those who follow him and live true to his words, but he doesn't just tell us not to be afraid. He says to us: 'Follow me, and the darkness will seek to overwhelm you too, but trust me: I am going to live true to God, and let the darkness destroy me, and then I am going to transcend the worst that the darkness can ever do. I am with you and in you through that journey of the cross, and with me you too will transcend the power of death.'

Your Choice

The invitation is given again and again, to each of us, every day.

The Way is waiting to welcome us.
The cost is high.
How do you choose to respond?

> 'I am the Way, the Truth and the Life.'
> JOHN 14:6-7

9

Entering the Gospels in prayer

IF 'FOLLOWING JESUS' really means trying to take his values and attitudes as the guide for our own choices and actions, if it means choosing to do the more loving, the more life-giving, the more Christ-like thing in every situation, however we might feel about it, then we are left with the problematic question of how would we know what this 'more loving, more Christ-like' choice would be.

We can ask the question 'What would Jesus do here?' but there is a difficulty with this: as human beings we have enormous capacity to delude ourselves, and when we ask what would Jesus do, or even 'what is God's will?' we are likely to convince ourselves that God would want pretty much what we were planning anyway. There is a better way to open ourselves to what the mind and heart of Christ would suggest in a particular situation, and that is to spend time praying with the gospels.

There are two time-honoured methods of doing this, which we will explore here. But whichever method you use, remember that what we are asking in this form of prayer is not: 'What happened, to whom and how?' Or even 'What did Jesus say or do at this point?' These questions are interesting, but they are ones that we address primarily in our heads, and with our intellects. They are the very valid subjects of bible study, but in scriptural prayer we are asking rather: 'What does this story mean to me, and how does it connect to the events and situations in my own life right now?' What does it reveal about the attitude Jesus would demonstrate in such a situation, and what values would shape his choices?

Imaginative meditation

Your imagination can be a wonderful ally in scriptural prayer. Some people distrust their imagination, and can't believe it could bring them closer to God. Yet how often did Jesus say: 'Imagine you are tending your sheep, baking your bread, sowing your crops... Now let me show you how these very things tell you something of what the Kingdom of God is like.'?

Try choosing a passage – perhaps a healing miracle or a parable – and just let your imagination take you to the scene. Notice what picture comes to mind, without trying to manufacture it. Notice who is there, and where you are yourself. Let yourself be wherever you truly find yourself. If you feel drawn to do so, engage in conversation with others at the scene, and especially with Jesus himself. What do you want to say? What do you feel Jesus might want to say to you? Does this scene bring to mind any connection with what is going on in your daily life? Does this passage have anything to show you about where Jesus would stand in the situation you are reflecting on?

Don't make any judgements, either about yourself or others. Just notice what happens and how you feel, and let those responses rest in the stillness of your prayer. Then take a moment to reflect on the experience, and on what you feel this prayer has been about for you. How are you going to move on in this situation in the light of this prayer? Is there anything further you would want to express to God now, after your time of reflection?

Lectio divina

Another ancient method of scriptural prayer is called lectio divina, which involves reading a short passage of scripture, noticing whether any word, or phrase or image especially speaks to you, taking time to meditate on what that fragment means to you, then letting what you have noticed turn into action in your life. To use this method in your normal everyday life, try the following process:

Begin the day by reading a passage of scripture (for example, part of the day's reading if you use a lectionary, or perhaps one of the daily bible reading guides that are available, or just simply choose a passage at random).

Notice whether any phrase or word or image or thought leaps out at you and engages your mind.

Reflect on that small fragment as you go through the

day. Whenever you have a spare moment (for example, when you are stuck in a line of traffic, or taking a shower or walking the dog, or taking a coffee break), bring it to mind and let it soak deeper into your heart, asking the question: 'What does this passage mean for me today and how does it relate to my life situations?'

At the end of the day take a few minutes to reflect on the fruits of your prayer and bring your response to God in whatever way feels right for you.

Could this work for you?

Praying with scripture in these, or other ways, can help to shape our daily living in surprisingly powerful ways. We think we are trying to 'get inside' the scriptures, but what is actually happening is that the scriptures are getting inside us, and gradually shaping our own attitudes and values so that they come closer to the mind and heart of Jesus.

> 'An unreflected life is not worth living.'
>
> SOCRATES

Wisdom comes from experience, but only when that experience has been reflected upon, and its fruits harvested.

10

Can my life make any difference?

I WAS ONCE travelling home on a Sunday in a train full of students returning to college after a weekend at home. One of them, sitting right next to me, was doing an assignment. She had been asked to think of what mattered to her in her choice of a career. She had lots of points, including job satisfaction, using her gifts, and earning a good salary. But right at the top of her list, and way ahead of other considerations was the statement of desire:

'I want to make a difference.'

We all want to make a difference. Most people hope that when their lives are over, they will be leaving the world a little bit better place than it was when they arrived.

And just as surely, most of us don't really believe our lives can make a difference. We think we are too small to count. Too insignificant to have any impact on the big scheme of things. Too unimportant for our tiny voices to be heard.

Are we just kidding ourselves with our thoughts of changing the world?

'What can you do?' we ask ourselves resignedly, in

the face of gross injustice or the horror of other people's suffering.

But what if ... faith makes a difference!
What if it were true? What if every one of us matters – really matters?

A few thoughts to ponder ...

This whole universe, with its trillions of galaxies, began as a tiny speck of concentrated energy, smaller than a grain of salt.

When you were first conceived, you were just a single cell, a mere pin-point of life, barely visible to the naked eye, but packed full of the potential for everything you would ever become, every action, choice and relationship.

You are just a drop in the ocean, but without you the ocean will not become an ocean.

You are just a grain of sand, but you are a grain of sand that tips the scales.

You are just a drop of dew that soaks into the earth and is gone by noon, but that drop of dew brings life to the seed that grows in the earth.

You are only one, but the Power of One is greater than you dare to dream.

One is not Nothing.

One makes a difference.

Your choices can tip the scales of humanity a little

bit more towards goodness and truth, if that is your desire.

But how?

To be a person of faith is to believe that you can make a difference and to work at making that happen.

It's about turning the ideal into the real. And we get to do that in the small things that happen every day.

We have a choice about those thoughtless comments, destructive put-downs, sarcastic rejoinders, times when we walk past a needy neighbour without offering help, times when we say nothing to challenge an injustice.

These things happen every day, and they are in our own power to change.

Just as surely, we can choose to offer an encouraging comment when we might have said nothing, to give time and a listening ear when someone close to us is hurting, to take some small step to do what we can – to slow climate change, to live more simply, to speak a word of tolerance and understanding where there is strife. There are opportunities for these things every day, and they are ours to use, or not to use.

The currency of change is in our own back pockets.

A person of faith is one who chooses to spend that currency, moment-by-moment, by making ordinary choices that tip the scales towards the greater good.

What do you *think?*

Do you want to make a difference?

Do you believe you can?

Take time to notice the choices you actually make today, the ways you choose to react to others, the words you choose to say? This is the currency of change. How do you feel about how you want to spend it?

> 'Ideals are like stars.
> You can never reach them.
> But you can use them to help
> you plot your course.'
> ANDRÉ GIDE

11

Faith is as faith does

IMAGINE THIS SCENE: John the Baptist, Jesus' friend and kinsman, is in prison because he has fallen foul of the authorities. From his prison cell he hears about all that Jesus is doing and wonders, is this man really the promised Messiah, or are we still waiting for another to appear? He sends out his own disciples to ask Jesus face to face. The answer comes back – not a simple Yes or No, but this: go back and tell John what you have seen – blind people seeing again, lame people walking, people with contagious disease cleansed, the deaf hearing again and the dead being raised to new life, and, above all, the poorest of the poor are being given good news, that they are worth everything in God's eyes and are sure of God's special blessing and care. (Matthew 11: 2-5)

This incident reminds me of a sermon I once heard in an urban church in a poor part of town. The preacher asked: 'Suppose a stranger were to come to you today and stop you in the street, and ask you "Where might I find Jesus of Nazareth?" What would you say?' There were a few murmured suggestions from among the congregation. Some would send the seeker to the nearest church, or maybe even the cathedral.

The preacher went on. 'Yes, of course you might find

him in a church, but maybe no more and no less there than anywhere else. What about the local hospital, where dedicated medical staff are tending the same people Jesus once tended? What about the schools where devoted teachers are nurturing young minds? What about those who are working to get a fairer deal for the poorest among us? And what about the ordinary homes along your street, where men and women are looking out for their neighbours and caring for their children and elderly relatives?'

Where do you see these things happening?

Jesus invites John to decide for himself who Jesus is, not on the basis of what people say they believe about him, but because of the effects he has, because of what he is doing. If you want to know what kind of a tree is in front of you, look at its fruits, not its botanical name. If you want to know where Jesus is now, look around you, not at the statements of a creed, but at the ways in which his Spirit is working in our lives today.

Faith is as faith does. To profess faith in Jesus and in the God he calls Abba, is to allow that Spirit to flow through our own lives and prompt and guide us to be present for others in the way that Jesus models for us. We can practise this in every situation we encounter, by choosing to do the more loving, the more life-giving, the more Christ-like thing next, in what we say and what we do.

Living like this is a great deal more demanding than merely affirming with our lips that we believe certain things about God, and about Jesus who incarnates the spirit of God in human form. It is easy to say a lot and do nothing. It is possible to do a great deal, and yet not to say anything, or assert anything.

A person of faith is someone who lives as though they mean what they say they believe and strives to be more like the one they say they follow.

Turning contemplation into action

I have a little oil lamp that was given to me by a friend, and is a constant reminder to me that a life of faith involves both contemplation and action.

The oil lamp has a wick, and the wick has two ends. If there is to be light, then one end of the wick has to remain submerged in the oil, and the other end has to be extended into the world. When both these conditions are in place, then, and only then, will there be a possibility of a flame bringing both warmth and light.

A person of faith is one who is called to bring a little bit more light and warmth into the world. To do this, it is necessary to remain rooted in a life of prayer and reflection, finding God in the ordinary things around us, and immersing ourselves from time to time into the deep silence of our hearts, where God is indwelling. But it is also necessary to be 'out there', burning with love and compassion, justice and peace, in a world that longs for light in its darkness and new ways forward through the labyrinth of contemporary life. If either of these is lacking, then our lives will not be channels of God's warmth and light.

As you look around you, where do you see fruits of the 'Jesus Tree' budding and sprouting?

Where do you see joy shining in the world?

Where do you see actions motivated by love?

Where would you direct someone who comes looking for the spirit of Jesus of Nazareth in your neighbourhood?

How would you feel if someone were to direct such a person to your door?

How is the wick in your oil lamp?

Just a question …

Life, and love, is for spending, not for saving. On what, or on whom, will you choose to spend yours?

> 'It is not anyone who says to me: "Lord, Lord," who will enter the Kingdom of Heaven, but the person who does the will of my Father in heaven.'
>
> MATTHEW 7:21

12

Journeying alone, journeying together

GETTING THE RIGHT balance between these two possibilities is always going to be a challenge as we journey in faith.

For some people, often those of a more introverted disposition, the tendency will be to see faith as something private and solitary – shaped by personal prayer and personal choices about how to live a God-centred life in the real world. The danger in this approach is that we may come to regard faith as a privatised means of obtaining an individual 'passport to heaven'.

For others, often the more extroverted by temperament, faith will be seen more as a community matter, expressed through public worship and in the embrace of an identifiable 'faith community', or church. The danger in this position is that public religious observance can become an end in itself, and lead to our neglecting the need for individual prayer and reflection

Both understandings are true and both dangers are real. Jesus warns us that the way of discipleship is narrow and to some extent we will have to walk it in single file. This means that we are invited to relate to God through personal prayer, which, by definition, is something we make in solitude.

However, the fruits of that prayer will not only affect ourselves, but those around us and the world as a whole. So faith is the journey of a single soul, but also a community matter.

The faith community

Like-minded people will always gather to share something of their lives with one another. This is especially true when it comes to questions of faith. A faith community is a group of people who gather regularly to express their faith in particular forms that they find helpful. This is traditionally known as 'going to church', but this is a misnomer, because 'church' isn't a place we go to, but a community of people we are, and this is as true in the streets as it is in the cathedral, as true on Monday as it was on Sunday.

'Church-going' is not necessarily the same thing as living a life of faith. It is possible to go to church services every week, or even every day, and still miss the point of what it means to follow Jesus. And it is possible to follow Jesus without going to church. Nevertheless, a faith community in some form is, I would suggest, an indispensible part of what it means to make a journey in faith.

We must each discover for ourselves where, and with whom, our faith community is to be found. For many it will be the traditional forms of church or chapel, but an increasing number of people who are trying to follow Jesus and live their lives in alignment with his values and teaching, are exploring other forms of building community that will nourish and guide them on this quest.

It really doesn't matter what we call our faith communities, or how they are organised, or where they meet. What matters is that we understand that we, as human beings, are born for community, and that we only have real meaning as individuals when we are in relationship – right relationship – with others.

'Soul-friends'

Our Celtic Christian forebears honoured a role they called the anam cara, which means a 'soul-friend'. A soul-friend is a person you trust enough to share some of the deepest matters of your heart with them, someone who will listen to what you share, without any kind of judgement, without trying to 'fix' anything, and without either flattering or criticising you. He or she will, however, listen lovingly to whatever you share, and then perhaps reflect back what seems to be stirring you most deeply, possibly also challenging you in firm but gentle ways or warning you if it appears you may be being untrue to your own deepest longings and intentions.

Soul-friends are a bit like midwives. They help to bring Christ to birth in your life and circumstances, but they only assist at the birth. They don't second-guess what form the 'baby' will take, and they let the birth happen in its own way and its own time. They are not there to take the pain away, but to help you deal with it. It is you who do the labouring, but they will rejoice with you at the miracle that is coming to pass.

How do you find a soul-friend? Look around you. Seek and you will find, and perhaps in places you didn't expect. A soul-friend is someone your soul can connect to and your heart can trust. One of the wisest soul-friends I know is a woman who left school at fourteen, and sees herself as a humble housewife, mother and grandmother.

What about you?

What does 'faith community' mean to you, and where do you find yours?

Do you have anyone you would see as a 'soul-friend'? If not, is this a relationship you would like to consider seeking out?

Perhaps others already see you as a soul-friend on their journey? How would you feel about that? Is there anything you could do to improve your listening skills?

> 'Where two or three meet in my name,
> I am there among them.'
> MATTHEW 18:20

13

I want to ask God ...

About why bad things happen?

It's the perennial question: if there is a God, why do catastrophes happen, and why do bad things happen to good people?

We inhabit a living planet. A planet without earthquakes, tsunamis and hurricanes would be inert. Life would certainly not have evolved on it. Change and upheaval go with the territory. Just as a child is not born into the world without labour and agony on the part of the mother, so life on earth comes into being, and keeps on renewing itself, through great contractions of the natural order, that often bring devastation in their wake. It's a different matter when we do harm to each other, or collude with systems that thrive on war and exploitation. The question is then not why does God allow it, but why do we do it, and what are we going to do about it? In his book When Bad Things Happen to Good People, Harold Kushner suggests that while our usual question is: 'God, why is this happening to me?' a more helpful question for a person of faith might be: 'God, this is happening to me. Now, how are you and I together going to deal with it in the most life-giving way, so that we can move on?'

About sin and eternal punishment?

Aramaic is a language, with many layers of meaning, that we tend to translate into just one or a few words in English, missing a great deal of the significance that Jesus would have understood and intended.

The word 'sin', for example, carries many layers of possible meaning. One of these is the reality that we often experience of 'missing the mark', of not getting things right, of compromising on our best, of failing to focus on what really matters.

Another layer of meaning is 'unripeness'. What if sin is like being an unripe fruit, bitter and unpalatable, compared to how it should be when it is fully ripe? What if humanity as a whole is still very 'unripe', still just teenagers in the scheme of things, or even 'terrible two-year-olds'?

As to eternal punishment, in the sense it has come down to us through tradition, I once visited Yellowstone National Park in Wyoming with a friend. We saw sulphur lakes there, belching forth reeking fumes, and looking like something out of Dante's Inferno. We gazed down on them in horror. I asked my friend: 'Can you imagine being here with someone who has done something really bad to you, and then picking them up and hurling them down into that?' 'No way,' she replied, grimacing in horror.

If she wouldn't, and I wouldn't, and you wouldn't, why do we think that God would?

About why Jesus had to die?

The question of why Jesus had to die is the arena of much debate and disagreement. A teenager once said to me: 'I know I don't always do things right, I can be selfish and mean, but even so, they're not pinning this man's death on me.' I had to concede that she was right, and that if we stop to think about it, we would be hard-pressed to say just how our misdemeanours, or even our fundamental lack of integrity, really caused God to hand Jesus over to the horror of crucifixion and whether we really believe that. Many ask, what kind of 'God' would that be? Surely the same kind of God we used to think was waiting to throw us into the sulphur lakes for any infringement of the Rules.

During his lifetime Jesus took on the forces of oppression and domination of his time, both secular and ecclesiastical, and exposed their hypocrisy and their bankruptcy. They didn't appreciate that then any more than they do now when people speak up for peace and justice. Today, if you speak up loudly and insistently enough you will almost certainly be silenced, and sometimes that silencing is brutal and violent.

One way of looking at why Jesus had to die might be this: in his lifetime he lived absolutely true to God's dream and God's values. He shone like a bright beam of light in a dark place, and the darkness didn't like it. He provoked the shadow side of humanity, and the shadow fought back by engulfing him and apparently destroying him. He constantly urged people: 'Live true to God and to yourself in every situation. The darkness may seek to destroy you, but I will show you that the worst that can happen can never destroy the spirit of who you are. I am living this truth, and I will die for it, and then I will transcend that destruction, and my spirit will flow free for ever.' Trust me, follow me, and don't be afraid.

What do you want to ask God?

We would all like to ask God questions, and we would all bring a different set of questions to the table. We have touched on just three such questions. There are many, many more. But are there really any answers?

What would you like to ask God?

So, what is faith?

Perhaps faith is not to know, but still to trust.

> 'Have patience with everything unresolved in your heart ... Live the questions now. Perhaps then, someday far in the future, you will gradually, without even noticing it, live your way into the answer.'
>
> RAINER MARIA RILKE,
> 'LETTERS TO A YOUNG POET'

14

I need to ask myself …

What really matters most to me?

I once happened to meet a young financial advisor who seemed to have his feet firmly on the ladder to success - until his life fell apart when his marriage ended. He had to move into a small rented apartment. Most of his savings were consumed by an acrimonious divorce settlement. And he only got to see his beloved two children on alternate weekends.

'I have learned so much in this past year,' he told me. 'I used to think I wanted a bigger house, expensive holidays, a fast car, and I told myself I wanted these as much for the family as for myself. Now I have come to understand that there are only two questions in life that really matter:

How will I spend my time,
And who with?'

I think that says in a sentence what people have written whole books about. Life is about how we spend the precious gift of the time we have been given, and about the relationships we make as we live that life.

Perhaps a life of faith is about choosing to spend our lives not just for ourselves but for the greater good, and about letting all our relationships be centred around our core relationship with God.

Am I trying to spend my life or save it?

All small children go through the 'my' and 'mine' stage. When they see something they want they claim it as 'mine' and vigorously defend their 'right' to it. They look at you in disbelief if you point out that nothing is actually 'mine' or 'ours' or 'theirs', but everything is gift. Most of us will learn the truth of this, but some people, of course, never do grow out of the 'my' stage and may even regard 'salvation' itself as a prize to be claimed and stored away.

Traditional religious practice can sometimes foster this desire to be 'saved', to get the coveted passport to heaven, to get our ticket for the celestial banquet and be counted among God's favoured ones. There is a temptation to regard faith as a stock market investment that we hope will pay the right dividends when the time comes.

But Jesus' life is 'spent', not 'saved'. He shows us through all his ministry and teaching, that we are to give ourselves away, not hoard ourselves and our gifts and resources.

There is a Christmas story of the 'fourth wise man', who set out with the others, carrying his gift to bring to the Christ-child, but as he journeyed he kept meeting people who were in desperate need, and so bit by bit he gave all his precious gift away to these needy people, and never did make it to Bethlehem. But did he deliver his offering or not? And did it matter that he didn't reach his intended destination?

These are questions we might need to ask ourselves as we reflect on whether faith is about being saved or being spent.

Am I really free?

We may live in what we like to call 'a free country' and enjoy freedom of speech and movement that our forebears have fought bitter wars to gain and maintain. But are we really free?

Many people would say that freedom means being able to do what you like as long as you don't harm others, or being able to organise your life as you wish without having to be accountable to anyone else.

A person of faith sees 'freedom' differently. Spiritual freedom is the ability to live in balance with all created things so that you can enjoy and use them responsibly without becoming dependent on them. It's about sitting lightly to what you think you 'own' so that if the need arises, you can let it go. It's about 'travelling light' along the pioneer pathways of life, so that your baggage doesn't make it impossible for you to move on.

Two employees worked for the same boss, whose

methods were sometimes dishonest and unscrupulous. One day one of them refused to carry out the boss's instructions, and he was fired. The other obeyed orders and was promoted. Afterwards the second employee said to the first: 'You fool. If you could only learn to obey his orders you wouldn't have to live so frugally now.' And the second replied: 'And if you could only learn to live frugally, you wouldn't have to obey his orders.'

Which one of them was free?

Are there any invisible chains around your life, that are holding you captive in situations, or compulsions that prevent you from growing and becoming the person God is dreaming you to be?

And you?

How do you feel about these questions?

Are there any questions you feel you need to ask yourself?

Can you let them arise in your prayer conversations with God?

> 'Learn from yesterday, live for today, hope for tomorrow. The important thing is not to stop questioning.'
>
> ALBERT EINSTEIN